Dea

I hope you are enjoying
your new school and home.
your classmates and I have
missed you so much.
We just want to let you
know that we think about
you and pray that you
and your family be blessed
always.

Love,

Mrs. Cechetto ♡

P.S. I hope you enjoy
this book. I know
you loved these car
books. I hope you
don't have this book already

McLAREN
ELVA
ELVA

26

BY KAITLYN DULING

EPIC

BELLWETHER MEDIA ››› MINNEAPOLIS, MN

EPIC BOOKS are no ordinary books. They burst with intense action, high-speed heroics, and shadows of the unknown. Are you ready for an Epic adventure?

This edition first published in 2024 by Bellwether Media, Inc.

No part of this publication may be reproduced in whole or in part without written permission of the publisher. For information regarding permission, write to Bellwether Media, Inc., Attention: Permissions Department, 6012 Blue Circle Drive, Minnetonka, MN 55343.

Library of Congress Cataloging-in-Publication Data

Names: Duling, Kaitlyn, author.
Title: Mclaren Elva / by Kaitlyn Duling.
Description: Minneapolis, MN : Bellwether Media, 2024. | Series: Cool cars | Includes bibliographical references and index. | Audience: Ages 7-12 | Audience: Grades 2-3 | Summary: "Engaging images accompany information about the McLaren Elva. The combination of high-interest subject matter and light text is intended for students in grades 2 through 7"--Provided by publisher.
Identifiers: LCCN 2023001649 (print) | LCCN 2023001650 (ebook) | ISBN 9798886875010 (library binding) | ISBN 9798886876895 (ebook)
Subjects: LCSH: McLaren automobiles--Juvenile literature. | Grand Prix racing.
Classification: LCC TL236.15.M35 D85 2024 (print) | LCC TL236.15.M35 (ebook) | DDC 629.222/2--dc23/eng/20230113
LC record available at https://lccn.loc.gov/2023001649
LC ebook record available at https://lccn.loc.gov/2023001650

Editor: Rachael Barnes   Designer: Jeffrey Kollock

Printed in the United States of America, North Mankato, MN.

TABLE OF CONTENTS

AN OPEN-AIR DRIVE »

A breeze blows. The sun shines down.
A McLaren Elva cruises down the open road.

This **supercar** has no roof and no windows. Drivers can enjoy the outdoors from inside the car!

ALL ABOUT THE ELVA »

BRUCE MCLAREN RACING IN 1963

McLaren began in England in 1963. Bruce McLaren started the company to build and race **Formula One** cars.

McLaren grew to make fast cars for the road, too. The 720S and F1 are famous **models**.

720S

⦿ WHERE IS IT MADE?

WOKING, ENGLAND

EUROPE

The Elva was announced in 2019. It had a limited run. Fewer than 150 were built. Bruce McLaren designed similar cars in the 1960s. The Elva is more powerful and much faster.

YEAR FIRST MADE 2020

$ COST starts at $1,690,000

 # HOW MANY MADE 149

FEATURES

exhaust barrels

carbon fiber body

deflector

The Elva was designed without a windshield!
It is the lightest road car ever made by McLaren.
This makes it faster.

The Elva can reach 124 miles (200 kilometers) per hour in 6.8 seconds. McLarens are record-setting cars!

WINNER'S CIRCLE

McLaren is known for building some of the top Formula One race cars. McLaren cars have won over 180 races!

FORMULA ONE
RACE CAR DRIVER
LANDO NORRIS

PARTS OF THE ELVA »

The Elva has a powerful **V8 engine** and a seven-speed **dual clutch automatic transmission.**

Four **exhaust barrels** give the car a loud growl. Everyone can hear it coming!

 ENGINE SPECS

TWIN-TURBO V8 ENGINE
»

TOP SPEED **203 miles (326 kilometers) per hour**

 0-62 TIME **2.8 seconds**

 HORSEPOWER **804 hp**

The name Elva comes from *elle va* in French. This means "she goes." The Elva is always on the go!

The Elva has a smooth, **carbon fiber** body. There are only three main pieces.

CARBON FIBER

SIZE CHART

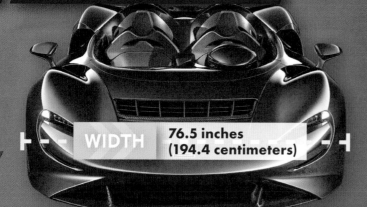

WIDTH	76.5 inches (194.4 centimeters)

A **deflector** on the front directs air up and over the car. This protects the driver and passenger from roaring winds.

DEFLECTOR

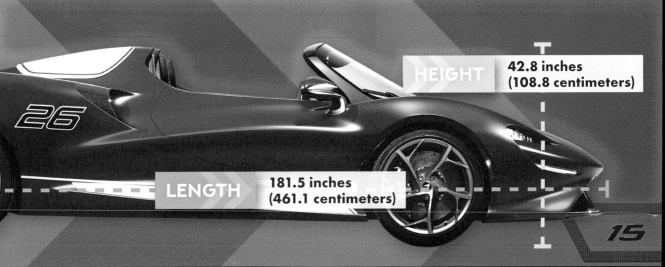

HEIGHT 42.8 inches
(108.8 centimeters)

LENGTH 181.5 inches
(461.1 centimeters)

Elva owners could choose to add a windshield. They could also choose the car's paint colors, wheels, and more.

FLYING DOWN THE ROAD

The Elva has special doors. Each one attaches to the car with a single hinge. They open upwards like wings.

Another option was a real gold **heat shield**. This fancy feature is hidden inside the engine!

Some drivers wanted to race the Elva
on a track. A **racing harness** could be
put in the car instead of a regular seat belt.

Passengers may get wet when it rains.
At least the Elva's seats are **waterproof**!

WATERPROOF SEATS

19

THE ELVA'S FUTURE »

McLaren plans to keep making supercars. But new McLarens will have different engines. Some will run on **electricity**. Many of the new cars will be **hybrids**. Future McLarens will be better for Earth!

GLOSSARY

carbon fiber—a strong, lightweight material used to strengthen things

deflector—a panel on the front of the Elva that directs wind up and over the car

dual clutch automatic transmission—a car part that has two clutches and changes gears automatically; a clutch is the part of a car that moves power from the engine to the wheels.

electricity—power that is carried through wires and used to run machines

exhaust barrels—pipes used to direct gases from a car's engine out and away from the car

Formula One—a type of car racing

heat shield—a piece of metal used to keep a car's body and other parts from getting too hot

hybrids—cars that use both a gasoline engine and an electric motor for power

models—specific kinds of cars

racing harness—a kind of seat belt with multiple straps

supercar—an expensive and high-performing sports car

V8 engine—an engine made with 8 cylinders arranged in the shape of a "V"

waterproof—not letting water through

TO LEARN MORE

AT THE LIBRARY

Adamson, Thomas K. *McLaren 720S*. Minneapolis, Minn.: Bellwether Media, 2023.

Orr, Tamra. *McLaren GT*. Minneapolis, Minn.: Kaleidoscope, 2022.

Smith, Ryan. *McLaren*. New York, N.Y.: AV2, 2021.

ON THE WEB

FACTSURFER

Factsurfer.com gives you a safe, fun way to find more information.

1. Go to www.factsurfer.com.

2. Enter "McLaren Elva" into the search box and click 🔍.

3. Select your book cover to see a list of related content.

INDEX